THE LITTLE BOOK OF

Kindness

A gift to bring hope and happiness

Lois Blyth

CICO BOOKS
LONDON NEW YORK

For Aliénore, Benjamin, and Oliver

Published in 2012 by CICO Books
An imprint of Ryland Peters & Small Ltd

20–21 Jockey's Fields   519 Broadway, 5th Floor
London WC1R 4BW   New York, NY 10012

www.cicobooks.com
10 9 8 7 6 5 4 3 2 1

A CIP catalog record for this book is available from the Library of Congress and the British Library.

ISBN: 978-1-908862-03-7

Printed in China
Editor: Marion Paull
Designer: Ian Midson

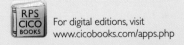

For digital editions, visit
www.cicobooks.com/apps.php

"Do it that very moment!
Don't put it off—don't wait.
There's no use in doing a kindness
If you do it a day too late!"

CHARLES KINGSLEY (1819–1875), ENGLISH NOVELIST

Introduction

The joy of writing a book on kindness is that it can be based only on personal stories. Kindness is not a place or a thing—although places can have a special niche in our memory, and things may be gifts of kindness; kindness can exist only when one person chooses to act with heart toward another. It is such a gentle and quiet quality and yet it is the stuff that glues humankind together.

I made some unexpected discoveries while writing this book:
• That people find it hard to remember their own acts of kindness. When it feels natural to give, people can no more remember being kind than they remember breathing. It is those who receive the kindness who remember the gift.
• That random acts of kindness are the most memorable—and that the unexpected kindness of a stranger can make us feel blessed and special.
• That kindness is a feeling rather than an event. Many people associate life events with memories of people being kind, but may not be able to remember the detail of the kindness.
• That the most profound experiences of kindness take place when

we are at our most vulnerable—when we are in trouble, when we are traveling, or when we are ill or in distress.

• That sometimes, to receive kindness means taking a risk—the risk of showing our feelings, or letting go of control, or putting our trust in a complete stranger in unfamiliar circumstances.

• That a kindness can lead to a bond of trust between people that transforms our perception of the world.

• That the smallest gesture can have the most profound power.

Genuine kindness is a gift indeed. It is offered with good heart, with the receiver rather than the giver in mind. When we nurture our capacity for kindness, we gladden our hearts and we take more notice of those around us. But the true magic of kindness is that it has the power to transform the giver more than the receiver, even if the kindness is proffered out of duty rather than good heart.

This little book is a celebration of kindness in all its forms and recognizes it as the kernel that lies at the heart of other human values, such as compassion, forgiveness, love, friendship, hope, generosity, happiness, and gratitude.

If someone has given you this book, the chances are they are acknowledging your kindness and the difference that you have made to their world.

The kindness principles: how to be kind

The history of kindness is as old as mankind. Aristotle wrote about it as long ago as 320 BC. It is considered to be one of the seven virtues.

As young children, most of us are taught to be kind: to treat others as we would like to be treated ourselves; to put others' needs ahead of our own; to say please and thank you.

There are as many kindness principles as there are ways to be kind, but here are the ones that we may overlook from time to time:

1. As far as possible, give from the heart—and when that is not possible, pretend that it is
2. Don't patronize those you are kind to
3. Always think yourself into the other person's shoes
4. Be aware of, and thank, those who are kind

5. Spend time with those who are lonely
6. Be courteous to all
7. Pay it forward—by paying for or helping someone else
8. Treat others as you would wish to be treated yourself
9. Find it in your heart to forgive
10. Smile through adversity
11. Give of yourself without expectation of anything in return
12. Be kind to yourself, also

One of the natural laws of kindness is that it is not necessarily mutually reciprocal—but kindness will come back from another source. That is the beauty of kindness—it is forever making new connections and binding us to one another.

Kindness is contagious —pass it on!

Kindness is a form of magic. The smallest act of kindness can have immense power. A kind gesture can transform a negative into a positive, a warm smile can lead to friendship or create a sense of belonging, a listening ear can offer hope where there was despair. The message that we should "Be kind to our enemies" encourages people to be dis-arming. It reminds us that we are all part of the same world. When we are kind to one another, a kind of alchemy takes place. The energy changes. The giver and the receiver feel good about themselves. The recipient of the kindness has a desire to be kind to others also—and so the magic spreads and the energy continues.

Act of Kindness
Putting others before yourself

"Tenderness and kindness are not signs of
weakness and despair but manifestations of
strength and resolution."

Kahlil Gibran (1883–1930)

"No act of kindness, no matter how small,
is ever wasted."

Aesop

Kindness opens doors

Some years ago, a young woman who I will call Angela was on a train leaving Waterloo Station in London, England. The whistle had blown and the train was about to pull away from the station when she saw a man running, trying to catch it. She threw open the door and helped him in.

After he had caught his breath and expressed his gratitude, they got chatting. He was American and it turned out he worked for a very famous chart-topping singer, who was at the peak of his fame. He was on his way to check out the next concert venue and to confirm the press schedule.

By the end of the two-hour train journey he had offered her a job working for the singer. She took unpaid leave from a good job with a bank to join the tour. As well as having a fantastic time and loving her job, she had the bonus of meeting famous people, having a backstage pass at concerts, and being transported in a chauffeur-driven limousine.

All because she had reacted fast and opened a door to help someone!

"Do all the good you can, and make as little fuss about it as possible."

CHARLES DICKENS (1812–1870)

The kindness of strangers

Have you ever experienced an unexpected act of kindness from a stranger? At a moment of desperation someone has appeared who has made all the difference, and has then disappeared from your life just as swiftly. Unexpected kindness can feel like a miracle. We are left full of gratitude—but perhaps unable to thank the person directly.

During moments of crisis, it seems we are more likely to experience unexpected generosity of spirit from people motivated solely by a desire to be kind or helpful to someone who is in distress. This may lead us to realize that kindness is an energy exchange. The person you are kind to may not be able to reciprocate directly to you, but the joy of it is they may be more motivated to give, and be kind, to others. It is one of the natural laws.

The Kindness of Strangers is a blog that was created in an attempt to fulfill a promise made by a woman called Betsy to a stranger 25 years ago. Spotting her broken-down car on the side of a rural highway in upstate New York, a man, who could have very easily kept on driving, stopped to offer assistance. He spent an entire afternoon helping her to get back on the road, accepting only a thank you in return, and "a promise that I would help someone else along the way." On April 3 2010, Betsy decided, "It is time I fulfilled that promise. I am making a commitment to be kind to a stranger at least once a day for a year."

And she did it. Her blog can be read at: www.oneyearofkindness.blogspot.com

> "Always, Sir, set a high value on spontaneous kindness. He whose inclination prompts him to cultivate your friendship of his own accord, will love you more than one whom you have been at pains to attach to you."
>
> JAMES BOSWELL (1740–1795), *The Life of Samuel Johnson*

Going out of your way

A teenager in Devon, England, had worked hard all summer to buy himself a moped. Not long after he brought it home, it was stolen and later found thrown in the river. The young man was left stunned by the theft and with no direct way of traveling to school to take crucial exams.

But he was even more shocked by what followed. A pensioner, who had read his story in the local paper, came into the cafe where he worked and gave him the money to buy a new one. She told him she had been moved almost to tears by his story and couldn't believe what had happened, and she wanted to help. But she didn't want any fuss.

The young man was overwhelmed by her generosity and deeply struck by the contrast of how one person could go out of the way to do something so unpleasant while another would go out of the way to put things right.

He bought a new moped with the money and has since got to know his benefactor, who, he says, is a very loving and special person. Her kindness has brought its own benefit—he now keeps in touch with her and has arranged to do some gardening for her, too.

> "Choose being kind over being right, and you'll be right every time."

RICHARD CARLSON (1961–2006)

> "I have never met a person whose greatest need was anything other than real, unconditional love. You can find it in a simple act of kindness toward someone who needs help."

ELIZABETH KUBLER-ROSS (1926–2004)

Act of Kindness

Smiling at others and showing them warmth

Kindness is good for you

It's official. Kindness is good for your health. Scientific research suggests that there is a link between kindness and the hormone oxytocin. The production of oxytocin is triggered by the hypothalamus in the brain. This sends a message to the tiny bean-shaped pituitary gland, which releases the oxytocin into the blood stream so it can do its work.

But where does the hypothalamus get its messages from? And what is oxytocin for? It makes you feel good, and is also known as the "love" hormone, because it is generated by acts of love and touch. Every time we kiss,

hug, make love, stroke the dog, or just touch someone's hand, we stimulate oxytocin production and start to feel better about the world. It triggers the production of milk in new mothers, and exciting new research suggests it plays an active part in healing heart muscle, too.

"No longer can we disconnect ourselves from our physical healing … The way we are feeling might just be the deciding factor in our recovery. And kindness makes us heal faster."

DAVID R. HAMILTON PHD, *Why Kindness is Good for You*

"Oh I love hugging. I wish I was an octopus, so I could hug ten people at a time."

DREW BARRYMORE (B. 1975)

The spongecake Samaritan

Baking is one of the oldest acts of kindness known to humankind. Somehow cakes, muffins, and cookies baked with heart rise higher, taste sweeter, and look lighter than anything you will buy off the shelf. Many people bake to celebrate, to show welcome, and to express their love for their family and friends. There is nothing like sharing food to bring people together, and nothing like a cake to make an occasion or a person feel special.

Cath Webb, a teacher from Cheshire, England, knows this more than most. She made the national news in the UK with her mission to bake a cake to give away every day for a year—just because she wanted to make people smile. Light, fluffy, and sweetly delicious

Victoria sponge cakes were baked daily and given to anyone who deserved a treat, from friends and family, to the local fire brigade, children at her school, nurses, a checkout operator—anyone who was in need of cheering up or had something to celebrate.

It started when a friend was diagnosed with cancer. Words seemed so inadequate that Cath decided to put all her feelings of love, care, and concern into baking her friend a cake. Her friend was very moved by her gesture—and Cath's mission began. Hundreds of eggs, bags of flour, and enormous quantities of preserve later, she is now known as the "spongecake" Samaritan. She kept a diary entry for each of her creations. Each beautifully baked cake was an act of kindness and a tribute to the person she baked for, whisked and blended with love and compassion as part of the filling.

"Just because an animal is large, it doesn't mean he doesn't want kindness; however big Tigger seems to be, remember that he wants as much kindness as Roo."

A.A. MILNE (1882–1956), *Winnie the Pooh*

Mahatma Gandhi

The power of non-violence

What greater kindness can leaders and politicians bestow upon their people than a personal philosophy based on respect for their fellow man and a political policy based on non-violence. Perhaps the greatest symbol of this ideal is the spiritual and political leader known to generations as **Gandhi** (1869–1948).

Mohandas "Mahatma" Gandhi is best known for his commitment to peaceful resistance and for his leading role in the ending of British rule in India in 1947. He had millions of followers in India and a profound influence around the world even within his lifetime. Not everyone agreed with his approach or his politics. His own life ended violently when he was assassinated by a fellow Hindu on January 30 1948 on his way to a prayer meeting. But that could not destroy the power of his approach.

"Mahatma" is a Sanskrit word, meaning "great soul."
"Satyagraha" means a non-violent way of protesting against injustice.

Many civil rights leaders, including Martin Luther King Jr, were inspired by Gandhi's non-violent approach to protest. He influenced Nelson Mandela. Albert Einstein considered him to be a role model. He has been a symbol of courage for Burmese leader Aung San Suu Kyi. As a symbol of strength and tolerance, Gandhi's influence extends far beyond his time or his country. The power of his words continues to inspire peace and kindness around the world.

"I am mindful that I might not be standing before you today, as President of the United States, had it not been for Gandhi and the message he shared ..."

BARACK OBAMA IN AN ADDRESS TO A JOINT SESSION OF THE PARLIAMENT OF INDIA, 2010

Feel-good Kindness

Much of kindness is to do with geography and opportunity.

When we tune in to a stranger's distress and realize we can help, it is perhaps an easy matter to take spontaneous action there and then. There is something about unexpected "feel-good" kindness. No responsibility is attached—it is a brief encounter that those involved will always remember with a warm glow.

But sometimes kindness is not a momentary choice, but rather an ongoing commitment and part of the job description. There are times when it is hard to be kind—times when kindness is mixed with duty or with suffering; and when no matter what we try to give, it doesn't seem to be enough. When kindness becomes a way of life, with little reciprocation, it transforms into something else that is bigger than the kindness itself. It becomes love in action and it comes from the heart.

"I expect to pass through this world but once.
Any good, therefore, that I can do or any kindness
I can show to any fellow creature, let me do it now.
Let me not defer or neglect it for I shall not pass
this way again."

ATTRIBUTED TO STEPHEN GRELLET C.1893

"Treat everyone you meet as if they are God in drag."

RAM DASS (B.1931)

Being true to your word

"It was during the first few days in my village. I had just moved into our cottage, my son was two, and I was on my own—packing boxes everywhere. I was excited, but, of course, anxious about my new life ahead. On about my third day, I was in the courtyard, and a lady passed by. We smiled at each other and had a very quick chat. She said welcome, and asked where I had come from. The next day,

when I got back from shopping, a note had been pushed through my door. "Hi, we met yesterday—I know you're on your own with a young child. If you ever need any help, here are my numbers. Please don't feel embarrassed to call, I'm here to help." That's it really—she was true to her word and has been a source of support for the last eight years. That small note made such a big impact on me—knowing that someone was there, at my doorstep, and offering their help freely."

Nichola

"The only people with whom you should try to get even are those who have helped you."

JOHN E. SOUTHARD

Act of Kindness
Babysitting for young neighbors for free

The role of gratitude

Kindness has a special partner. Gratitude.

The practice of kindness makes people feel surprisingly good about themselves. It is a habit that is easy to develop. The gift of thanks has the power to transform, also. Offering appreciation is in itself a kindness that can melt the most cynical of hearts. It is so much easier to continue being kind when we feel appreciated. We all know that kindness should be about giving, not receiving; and that the focus should be on others, not ourselves. But it is only human to want to feel valued.

"To give and receive are one truth.
I will receive what I am giving now.
To everyone I offer quietness.
To everyone I offer peace of mind.
To everyone I offer gentleness."

A COURSE IN MIRACLES

Be kind to yourself—you deserve it, too

Sometimes people forget that they need to befriend themselves. Until we care for ourselves, and until we are at ease with who we are, we will not be at peace, and we will not be free to give all of our heart to others. If we are hard on ourselves, we allow our experiences to harden our hearts.

"I began to see that in some way, no matter what subject I had chosen, what country I was in, or what year it was, I had taught endlessly about the same thing: the need for maitri (loving kindness toward oneself)."

PEMA CHÖDRÖN, TEACHER
AND BUDDHIST NUN (B. 1936)

The gentle art of gracious giving

When someone is in need, it is kinder to be gracious and to ask, "What would you like?" rather than to give that person what you think he or she needs. In that way, the giver offers choice and hope —even when a life feels completely out of control.

Sometimes, sending a short note to say, "I just want you to know I care …" is all that is needed.

The debt of kindness

Usually in life, it is easier to give than to receive. Being on the receiving end of kindness is not always comfortable. It can be hard to take from others when you are unable to give something in return.

- A lot of elderly people know this.
- Most people with a disability experience it.
- Those who have suffered illness or injury discover it.
- Many who have relied on others for practical or financial help will understand it, too.

So sometimes, those we try to help will resent our kindness. They may be unkind in return. In those moments when kindness is rebuffed, or unappreciated, we need to remember that the act of giving is not in itself the gift. Kindness has a greater purpose. It is about caring for our "kind."

The greatest kindness to someone who is vulnerable may be to ask how he or she is feeling, rather than to make assumptions about what that person may want or need.

Monday night is lasagna night

"A neighbor of mine was diagnosed with cancer, and I knew she was going through a really hard time. I wanted to help, but I didn't want to intrude. So I asked a friend, who had been through something similar, 'What's the nicest thing I could do, since I don't know her very well?'

My friend had a great suggestion: "Maybe you could offer to make her family a meal once a week. When I was having to undergo treatment, I found mealtimes to be really exhausting, so that would be a good one."

So I said to my neighbor, 'I really want to help you. If you can think of any way that I can, then please talk to me about it. A friend of mine said it was useful to her to have someone else prepare meals, and I would like to offer you that, if you think it would help you.'

I made a commitment to prepare supper for her family every Monday for six months, and they could tell me what they did and didn't like. But usually it was lasagna, because that was their

favorite. So my lasagna became famous, and we became friends, and Monday night became lasagna night!"

Eliza

Act of Kindness

Giving someone your last piece
of chocolate, even though you
had been saving it for later

The Dalai Lama

Kindness through compassion

Tenzin Gyatso is the 14th Dalai Lama and a Buddhist monk. He was born into a simple farming family and was given the name of Lhamo Dondrub before being found at the age of two. Tibetan Buddhists believe him to be a reincarnation of his predecessors and the Buddha of compassion. At the heart of all his teachings is the universal message that we all deserve to be happy, and that showing love and compassion to others is the route to kindness and contentment.

He describes loving-kindness as being the pathway to personal fulfillment. The ability to be kind is part of the life force within us. We need to be kind and show compassion—it is part of who we are. It transcends ignorance, aggression, and attachment, because it is impossible to be kind or compassionate and aggressive at the same time.

But the art of loving-kindness takes practice and self-discipline. If we do not practice it, and show it as often as we can, we may cause harm to ourselves and to others, because we will not be able to overcome our feelings of aggression, and we may not be able to put the essential needs of others before our own.

"This is my simple religion. There is no need for temples; no need for complicated philosophy. Our brain and our heart is our temple. The philosophy is kindness."

HIS HOLINESS THE DALAI LAMA (B.1935)

Making time for kindness

A lot of us spend our lives in a rush. We email instead of writing letters; we text messages instead of talking; we use voicemail instead of phoning people back. Most of the time that is okay; but it may also mean we have stopped paying proper attention to those

around us. Sometimes the greatest act of kindness is giving someone time to talk, and really listening to what they have to say.

"People often say, 'You look lovely, you have a lovely smile; you look great,' and think they are giving you compliments—but those are superficial things. They are very nice to hear, and they hit the surface, but it's all at face value. When someone takes the time to listen to you, that's what really counts."

Bella

"A kind friend is someone who is there for you in your darkest moments; who understands you—and reminds you of who you truly are."

Tanya

Act of Kindness
Welcoming new neighbors by taking them
a home-baked gift

A gesture of friendship

"My father was one of the kindest people I have ever known. Many years ago the local vicar was briefly arrested as part of a dawn raid by the police. As you can imagine, there was uproar and much speculation and gossip around the village, and the following Sunday at church the congregation was much smaller than usual. My father, who knew the vicar well, as he often read the lesson and helped with events, attended

the service as usual. However, when shaking hands with the vicar in the porch on the way out (as is the tradition,) he slipped him a bottle of very good red wine that he had brought with him specially and which he had been carefully concealing under his coat. It was a clear gesture of friendship, solidarity, and support at a time when these were in short supply and many stayed away. Kindness personified and a father to be proud of."

Louise

"One can pay back the loan of gold, but one dies forever in debt to those who are kind."

MALAYAN PROVERB

"Be kind to each other. It is better to commit faults with gentleness than to work miracles with unkindness."

MOTHER TERESA (1910–1997)

Making a contract
with kindness

You have to be careful with kindness. Being aware of the reason you are giving is important. Sometimes when you give, your intention to be kind may stem from a sense of duty, or from your need for approval, rather more than from a desire to offer a gift of help. And sometimes when you give, people just want more, and that can be difficult, too. If you reach a point where you can only feel good about yourself when you are being kind to others, then you probably need to stop for a while, and start being a little kinder to yourself.

Kindness comes in many guises, including compassion, patience, giving, generosity, friendship, trust, loyalty, gratitude, warmth, and forgiveness.

The more you give of these qualities, the more you will receive in return. But beware of the enemies of kindness: cynicism, doubt, hurt, suspicion, anger, self-interest, and selfishness. The more you give in to these traits, the more upset and hurt you will cause yourself.

"The greatest good you can do for another is not just to share your riches but to reveal to him his own."

BENJAMIN DISRAELI (1804–1881),
BRITISH PRIME MINISTER AND AUTHOR

Mother Teresa

Agnes Gonxha Bojaxhiu was born in Skopje, Serbia in 1910. Drawn to a religious life from a very early age, she left her home at the age of 18 to join the Sisters of Loreto in Dublin, Ireland. Just two years later, Sister Teresa, as she was known by then, began teaching at a convent school in Kolkata (Calcutta,) India. Greatly affected by the extreme poverty that she saw each day, she said she received "a calling within a calling" to leave the confines of the convent and devote her life to caring for the poorest of the poor. With just basic medical training and no funds, she set out to work in the slums. She was 38 years old and completely dependent on volunteers and financial donations. But her reputation grew and her work was recognized and supported.

Two years later, by which time she had been joined by a community of nuns and volunteers, and become known as "Mother" Teresa, she received permission to start her own order, The Missionaries of Charity. They looked after those who were starving, crippled, ill, and destitute, and their work and her reputation grew. A tiny

woman wrapped in a white sari with a blue border, Mother Teresa's face became recognizable around the world. She was a symbol of compassion, love, kindness in action—and a symbol of hope for those in crisis or marginalized by society. In 1979 she was awarded the Nobel Peace Prize. By the time she died in 1997, she had over one million co-workers in over 40 countries around the world. Princess Diana was one of her most prominent supporters.

"You will find Kolkata all over the world if you have the eyes to see."

MOTHER TERESA (1910–1997)

Never be cruel to be kind

Parenting is a difficult job to get right. It is full of apparent contradictions. The advice is endless—and often questionable. "You have to be cruel to be kind sometimes." "You are killing the child with kindness." Can either of these statements ever be true? Is cruelty ever justified? No, never. Can you really kill someone with kindness? It seems unlikely, unless the "kindness" is masquerading as something else—fear perhaps, or anger, or jealousy.

The only rules of kindness are to treat children with love and respect, and to help them to develop the same regard for others.

It is kind to give toddlers clear guidelines for behavior, and to teach them right from wrong.

It is kind to help young children to understand their skills and talents, and to learn to manage their emotions.

It is kind to encourage teenagers to think for themselves, and to give them a safe place to learn from their mistakes, while showing them how to take responsibility for their feelings and their actions.

When our children lose their way, it is also kind to help them to put things right, to regain their self-respect and have faith in the future—but never with cruelty.

> "Ignorant kindness may have the effect of cruelty; but to be angry with it as if it were direct cruelty would be an ignorant unkindness."

GEORGE ELLIOT (1819–1880)

Act of Kindness
Being spontaneously affectionate

A thank-you card that lasts for life

"A little girl comes to stay with us sometimes. She is just 9 years old. One day she gave me a little card, and inside it said: 'Whenever you are blue, just know that I am thinking of you.'

There was no particular reason for it. It was just a card that she wanted me to have, so that if ever I did feel sad, I could pick it up and be happy. It really touched my heart.

When someone takes the time to thank you for doing something that to you is just normal, it means a lot, because they are saying, 'You're really special and I thank you for being you'—and that is really kind."

Sarah

"You give but little when you give of your possessions. It is when you give of yourself that you truly give."

KAHLIL GIBRAN (1883–1930)

"Forget injuries; never forget kindness."

CONFUCIOUS

"How far you go in life depends on your being tender with the young, compassionate with the aged, sympathetic with the striving, and tolerant of the weak and strong. Because someday in your life you will have been all of these."

GEORGE WASHINGTON CARVER (C.1864–1943)

Money makes the world go round

Sometimes in life, people encounter financial difficulties. They will often soldier on in private, withdrawing from friends or falling out with loved ones, too proud to ask for help until it is too late. But sometimes, those who care about them will tune in, notice that something is wrong, and come up with a big gesture that makes a life-changing difference:

"Back in the 60s, older friends of my mum and dad's gave them the money they needed for the deposit on their first house. Without that help they would not have been able to afford to buy anything."

Naomi

"One day, completely unexpectedly, I received a check in the post from a client who felt I had done more work than I had invoiced for. Not only was it an incredibly generous thank you, she also funded the first holiday I'd had for a while."

Simon

"My cousin took over the sale of a friend's house and she got an extra $70,000 for it! I think this may come under The Most Profitable Act of Kindness!"

Neil

"I run my own business and some years ago had cashflow problems. I was in arrears with my mortgage and other bills, and had reached crisis point. But I didn't feel I could talk to anyone about it. Then my brother came to stay. I was very tense and irritable but he didn't rise to my bad temper. He could tell something was seriously wrong. The morning he left I found an envelope on the kitchen table. Inside was enough money to buy me some time with my repayments and a lovely letter. The money was a godsend—but the letter was of greater value, and I will keep it forever."

Gillian

Larry Stewart

American philanthropist Larry Stewart (1948–2007) was the original "Secret Santa." He came from a modest background and made his own way in life, earning a substantial fortune from cable television and long-distance communications. But even when he had made a lot of money, he remembered his beginnings, and what it felt like to be out of work. He had especially strong memories of being fired, just before Christmas, two years in a row, when he was in his very early 30s.

The second time it happened, he went to eat at a drive-in restaurant, feeling very down on his luck, and noticed a young woman washing cars outside. It was a bitterly cold day and she was wearing a very light jacket. The story goes that the sight of her working so hard for "nickels and dimes" made him reflect on his own situation and realize that things could be worse. When she washed his car, he gave her a $20 tip and she burst into tears of gratitude. That small sum had made a significant difference to her life.

From that time on, until a year before his death, he used to give away small amounts of cash, anonymously, and often in $100 bills, to those in need. The total amount he gave away is estimated to be $1.3 million. He also donated to community charities, but had great belief in giving spontaneously and directly to people who needed it, so that they did not have to ask anyone for help.

In his mid-50s he was diagnosed with cancer and began "training" other people to be Secret Santas before the due holiday season. Sadly, he died a year later, but the tradition lives on. Since then, Larry Stewart's humble generosity has inspired a whole movement.

Everyone needs a Secret Santa

"A couple of years ago my husband lost his job. We have two young children, and were struggling financially, but we were able to buy the basics. Just.

One morning I opened the front door to find a large box on the doorstep. Inside it were all kinds of delicious things we wouldn't normally be able to buy, such as olive oil, balsamic vinegar, really nice coffee, chocolates, and cookies. I felt like a child again—incredibly grateful, and intrigued to know who it was from.

It was two weeks before Christmas, and every morning for three mornings, I woke up to find a box of food on the doorstep. By the fourth morning I had started to believe in fairies again, and actually looked for another box! I was pretty certain that I knew who our generous benefactor was, but she didn't want me to know it was her, so we left it a secret.

What we really appreciated more than anything was the care with which she had chosen the contents of the boxes. She had made the

giving and receiving so special that instead of being charity, it felt like an exciting treat!

These days we are able to give back to her in quiet ways, but we will never forget that sense of being looked after—and her incredible kindness."

Marie

Act of Kindness
Keeping your promises

Kindness is still kindness,
whatever the motive

"My boyfriend had been out of work for some time. He was very low and was feeling angry with the world. He is good at carpentry and so I asked him to come with me to help decorate a local shelter for the homeless. He joined me very reluctantly, saying he didn't believe in charity and had better things to do with his time.

Of course, it was a day full of banter and he got chatting to some of the people at the shelter while he worked, who were so grateful to him for putting in a few hours to help out. Receiving such appreciation really lifted his spirits and he offered to come back and share some of his skills. Life suddenly felt full of possibilities again. As he said later, he hadn't realized how much he would get out of helping others. It was hard to know who was being more kind to whom!"

Lucy

"It is futile to judge a kind deed by its motives.
Kindness can become its own motive. We are made
kind by being kind."

Eric Hoffer (1902–1983)

Act of Kindness
Phoning your mother-in-law for a chat
(even when you don't really
feel like it)

The ripple effect

Kindness is one of the essential teachings of every spiritual philosophy in the world since time began. It is a survival skill. Kindness has always spread naturally, binding friend to friend and protecting us from our foes.

But only in the electronic age has kindness become a movement. The Internet is alive with good heart and powerful intentions as people around the world find ways to "Practice random kindness and senseless acts of beauty."

This wonderful phrase is accredited to Anne Herbert, an American, who is said to have written it on a table mat in a restaurant. Others copied it, bestselling writer Jack Kornfield included her story in his writing, and since then it has spread, literally, around the world, inspiring generous actions and good-hearted gestures in its wake.

"Carry out a random act of kindness, with no expectation of reward, safe in the knowledge that one day someone might do the same for you."

PRINCESS DIANA (1961–1997)

"Remember there's no such thing as a small act of kindness. Every act creates a ripple with no logical end."

SCOTT ADAMS (B. 1957)

The role of gratitude

Have you had a kindness shown?
Pass it on;
'Twas not given for thee alone,
Pass it on;
Let it travel down the years,
Let it wipe another's tears,
'Til in Heaven the deed appears—
Pass it on.

"Pass It On"
Henry Burton (1840–1930)

There is a story behind the creation of Henry Burton's verse. A young boy called Mark Guy Pearse was once making the long journey home from boarding school by boat when he discovered that he did not have enough money for the fare. He was extremely anxious and upset and waited in trepidation for the boatman to reach him. Recognizing his honest distress, the boatman reached into his pocket and paid the rest of the fare with his own money.

Before Mark could thank him, the man said, "Remember what happened today, and if ever you ever come across someone else in the same situation, pass this kindness on."

Many years later, Mark Guy Pearse was on a railway platform waiting for a train when he spotted a boy in tears. He asked him what was wrong and the boy sobbed, "I haven't any money left for my fare." Mark Guy reassured him, "Don't cry. I'll buy the ticket for you." As they walked together along the platform, he remembered his promise to the boatman and told the boy to pass this kindness on.

Mark Guy Pearse (1842–1930) was a Cornish Methodist preacher. Dr Henry Burton was Mark Guy Pearse's brother-in-law. The story inspired him to write his hymn, "Pass it On."

Danny Wallace's Karma Army

Back in 2002, British comedian Danny Wallace put an advert in a newspaper. It just said, "Join me." All the applicants needed to do was to register and send a passport photo. As Danny says on his website, "No one knew what they were joining. Or who they were joining. Or really, why they were joining. But join they did!"

The problem was, he didn't know why they were joining either! He needed to create a cause.

So he asked people to commit to performing one random act of kindness a week—preferably for a stranger—and on a Friday. The initial gathering grew into a network of people who were motivated to be spontaneously nice just for the sake of being nice. And so Danny Wallace's "Karma Army" and the Good Friday movement were born—a random act of humor turned into something that was pure genius.

Danny collected all the stories of kindness and published them in a book called *Join Me*. As he puts it, "It's not a cult, it's a collective!"

The Karma Army still marches on, and has gathered its own momentum around the world.

www.joinme.co.uk

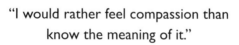

"I would rather feel compassion than know the meaning of it."

St Thomas Aquinas

"The best way to cheer yourself up is to cheer someone else up."

Mark Twain (1835–1910)

Chain 124

A record-breaking medical chain of kindness took five months to run its course, and spanned America. In the process, Rick Ruzzamenti of Riverside, California and Donald Terry Jr of Joliet, Illinios, made history. They were the first and last people in a 60-person chain of 30 kidney donors and 30 transplants that was logged by the Kidney Donor Register as Chain 124. It began on August 15 and ended on December 20 2011.

In a medical adventure worthy of a Hollywood epic, Chain 124 was generated by Ruzzamenti's impulsive act of kindness. He simply decided one day that he wanted to donate one of his kidneys and called in to Riverside Community Hospital, California to find out how to go about it. His decision set in place a carefully coordinated chain of medical events and procedures that eventually saved 30 lives. Every donation and every operation was an individual story of kindness, benevolence, and love in action.

A longer version of this story was reported by Kevin Sack in the *New York Times* on February 19 2012 as "A string of kindness: 30 kidneys, 60 lives."

"The kindness I have longest remembered has been of this sort, the sort unsaid; so far behind the speakers lips that almost it already lay in my heart. It did not have far to go to be communicated."

HENRY DAVID THOREAU (1817–1862)

Michael Landy

"Acts of Kindness" is a project by artist Michael Landy, celebrating everyday generosity and compassion on the London Underground. He invites us to notice acts of kindness, however simple and small.

The artist explains, "Sometimes we tend to assume that you have to be superhuman to be kind, rather than just an ordinary person." So, to unsettle that idea, Acts of Kindness catches those little exchanges that are almost too fleeting and mundane to be noticed or remembered.

Landy defines kindness as going beyond yourself to acknowledge someone else's needs and feelings. Being kind to a stranger involves sharing that sense of connection with someone you don't know. "It's a gesture of trust between two people," he says. "There's a risk in that. They may just ignore you or take it the wrong way." It requires courage and acceptance on both sides.

The beauty of kindness is that everyone is capable of it. It costs nothing and it is easy to pass on.

"A hint of fragrance always clings to
the hand that gives roses."

CHINESE PROVERB

"Be kind whenever possible.
It is always possible."

HIS HOLINESS THE DALAI LAMA (B.1935)

Acknowledgments

With enormous gratitude for stories and kindnesses past and present: Rusty Ansell, Margaret Barron, Tanya Byron, Jane and Simon Colston, Florence Hamilton, Louise Hopkins, Katherine Howard, Pam Ives, Nicole "Kolly" Jones, Sue Lanson, Veron Lien, Laura and Atilio Loncar, "Pastor Norm" Mowery, Vanda North, Marion Ridgewell, Sharee Ryan, Jenny Summerton, Annabel Sutton, John and Lois Sutton, Richard Sutton, Nichola Vickers, Christina Volkman, Pat Watson, Sarah Woodger, and as always, Keith King.

For their great care, creativity, and the opportunity to write this book: Dawn Bates, Cindy Richards, and Clare Sayer at Cico Books.

Picture Credits

Copyright © Ryland Peters & Small: p18 Martin Brigdale; p22 Lucinda Symons; p24 Winfried Heinze; p28 Mark Lohman; p31 Martin Brigdale; p36 Carolyn Barber; p44 Vanessa Davies; p48 and p51 Carolyn Barber; p52 Laura Edwards

Used under licence from ShutterStock, 2012: p1 Gino Santa Maria; p3 NH; p7 fotohunter; p9 Yuri Arcurs; p11 l i g h t p o e t; p13 Kletr; p14 Bobo Ling; p16 Dmitry Lobanov; p21 Sylvana Rega; pp26–27 Anne Kitzman; p33 szefei; p34 Darren Baker; p39 Marina Dyakonova; p41 Matthijs Wetterauw; p42 Lana K' p47 pjmorley; p54 Junial Enterprises; p57 chinahbzyg; p59 Valentina R; p61 ouh_desire

Used under licence from iStockphoto, 2012: p63 mstay

Text Credits

Michael Landy's Art of Kindness project (see pages 62–3) is online at http://art.tfl.gov.uk/actsofkindness/about/

"Going out of your way" (see pages 14–15): this story was first reported in *The Sidmouth Herald*